Who Thought Learning Could be Fun

The Fun Book

Lucy Maisano

AuthorHouse™
1663 Liberty Drive
Bloomington, IN 47403
www.authorhouse.com
Phone: 1-800-839-8640

First published by AuthorHouse   05/05/2011

ISBN: 978-1-4567-3678-1 (sc)
ISBN: 978-1-4567-3677-4 (ebk)

Library of Congress Control Number: 2011901967

Printed in the United States of America

Any people depicted in stock imagery provided by Thinkstock are models, and such images are being used for illustrative purposes only.
Certain stock imagery © Thinkstock.

This book is printed on acid-free paper.

Name

A   A   A   A

A   A   A

A

a   a   a   a

a   a   a

A a   A a

Name _____

B B B B

B B B

B

b b b b

b b b

B b B b

Name _____

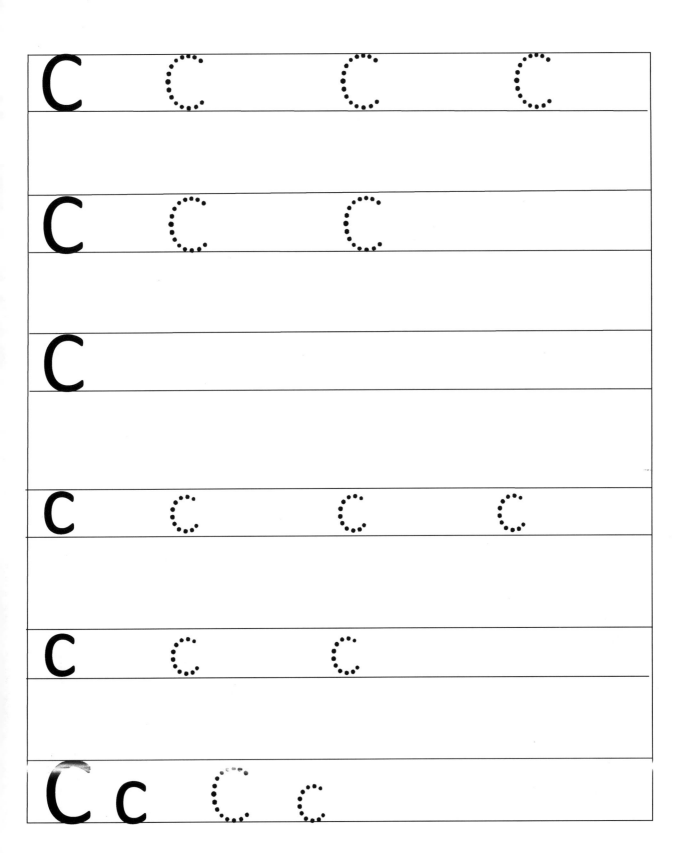

D D D D

D D D

D

d d d d

d d d

D d D d

Name _____

E   E   E   E

E   E   E

E

e   e   e   e

e   e   e

E e   E   e

Name _____

F   F   F   F

F   F   F

F

f   f   f   f

f   f   f

F f   F   f

Name _____

G G G G

G G G

G

g g g g

g g

G g G g

Name _____

H   H   H   H

H   H   H

H

h   h   h   h

h   h   h

Hh   Hh

Name _____

I   ⋮   ⋮   ⋮

I   ⋮   ⋮

I

i   i   i   i

i   i   i

I i   i   i

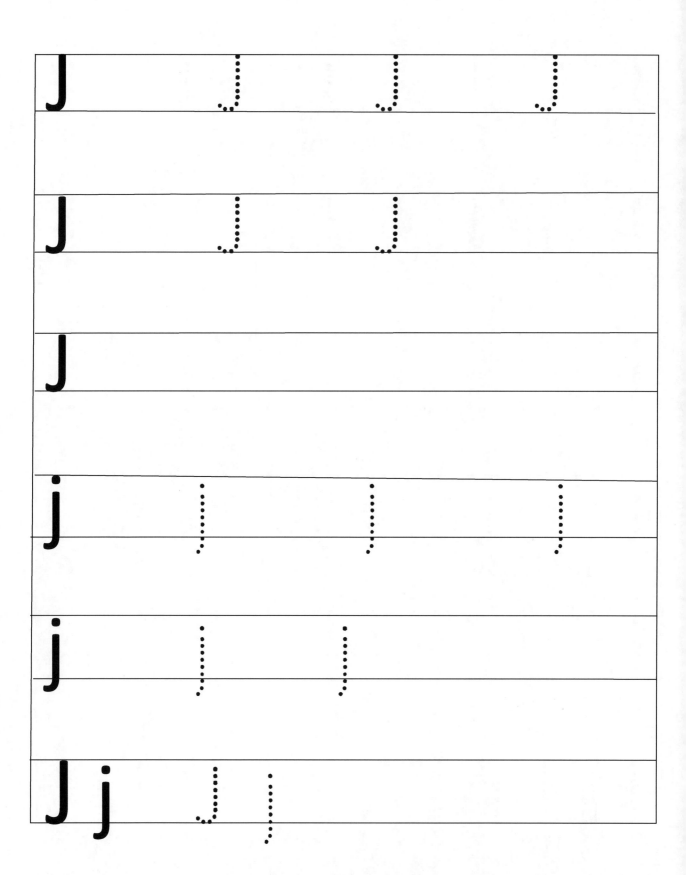

Name_____

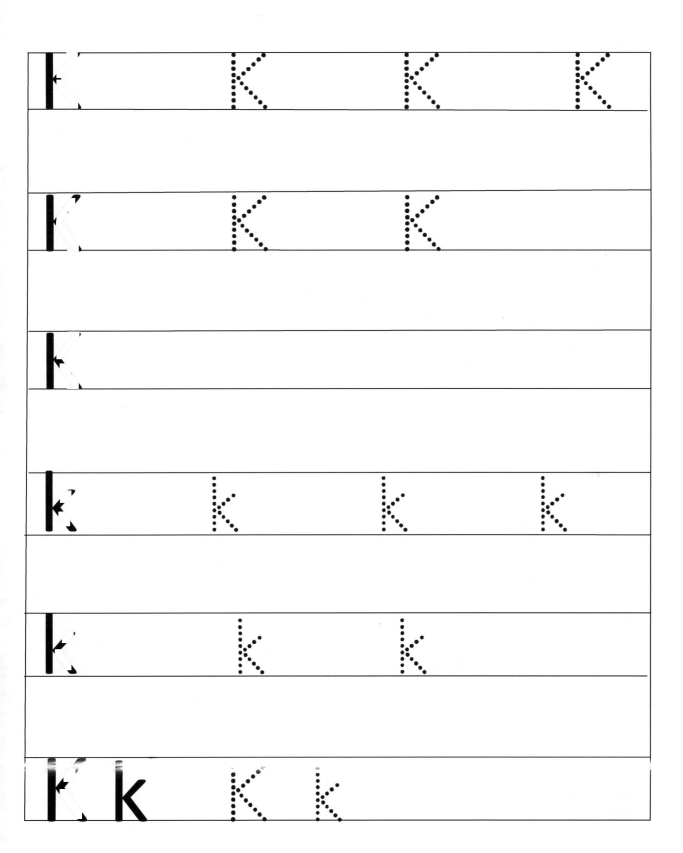

L   L....   L....   L....

L   L....   L....

L

I   I   I   I

I   I   I

L I   L...   I

Name _____

M · · M · · M · · M · ·

M · · M · · M · ·

M

m m m m

m m m

M m M m

Name _____

N N N N

N N N

N

n n n n

n n n

N n N n

Name

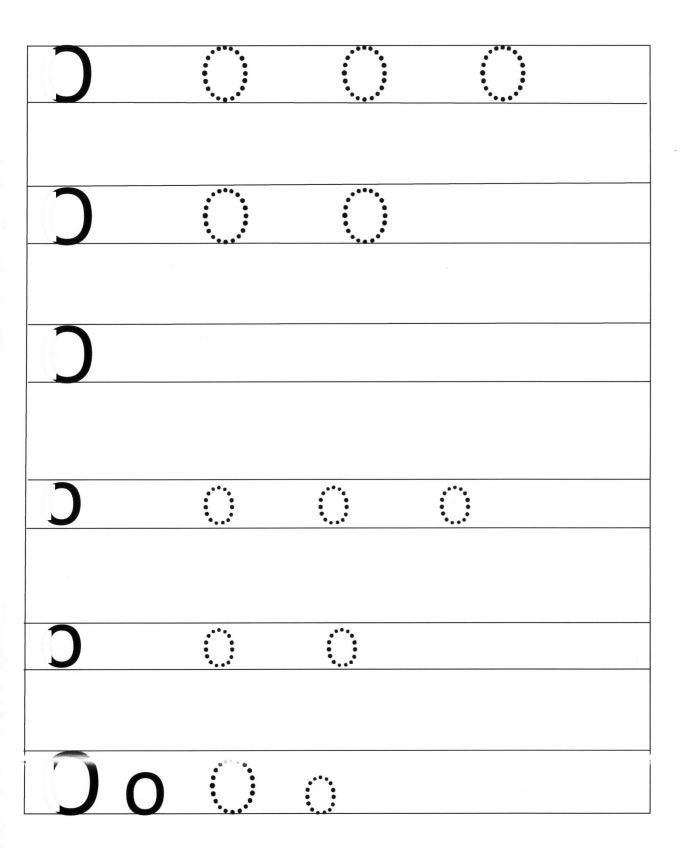

P   P   P   P

P   P   P

P

p   p   p   p

p   p   p

P p P p

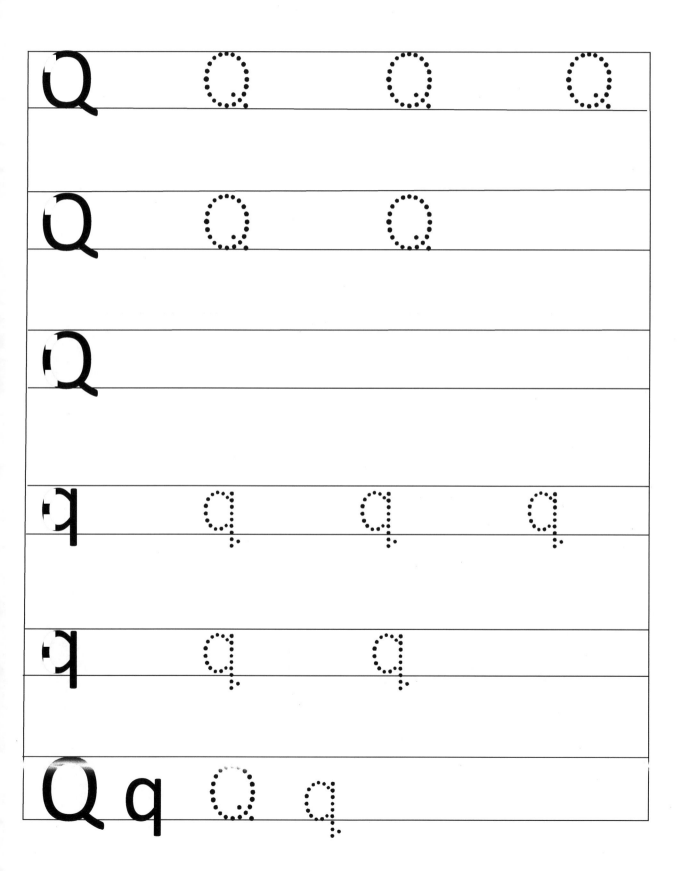

Name _____

R   R   R   R

R   R   R

R

r   r   r   r

r   r   r

Rr   Rr

S   S   S   S

S   S   S

S

S   S   S   S

S   S   S

S S   S   s

Name_____

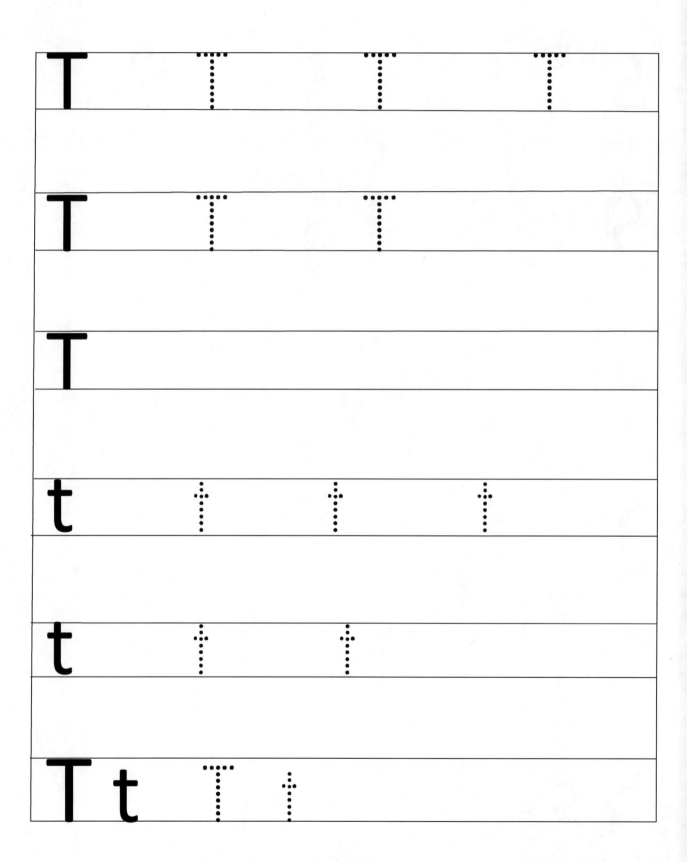

Name

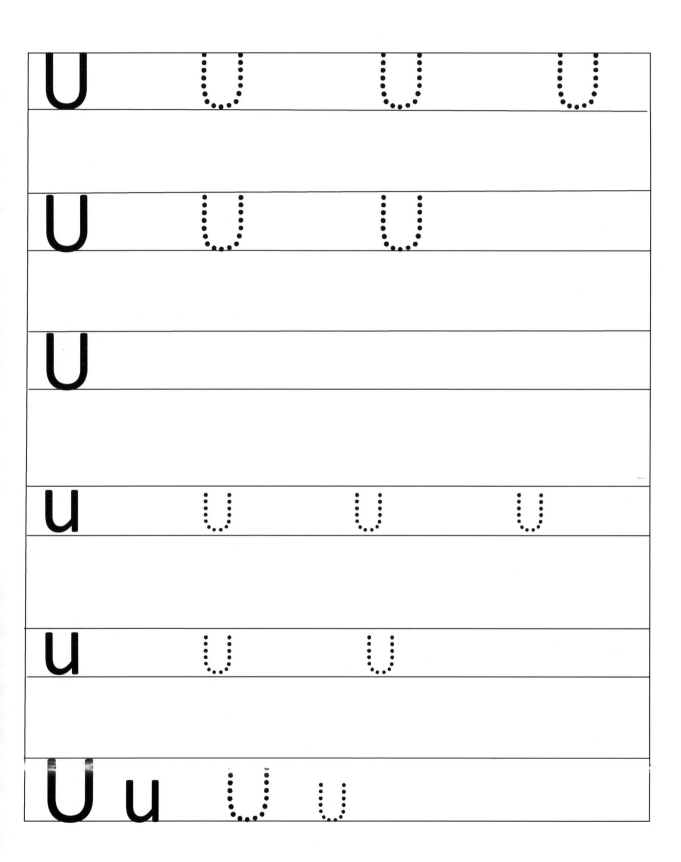

Name_____

V v v v

V v v

V

V v v v

V v v

V v v v

Name

W   W   W   W

W   W   W

W

W   W   W   W

W   W   W

W w W w

Name _____

X   X   X   X

X   X   X

X

X   X   X   X

X   X   X

X x   X   x

Name _____

Y   Y   Y   Y

Y   Y   Y

Y

y   y   y   y

y   y   y

Y y   Y y

Z z Z z

Z z Z z

Z

Z z z z

Z z z

Z z Z z

1   1   1   1

1   1   1   1

1   1   1   1

1   1   1

1   1   1

1

Name _____

2   2   2   2

2   2   2   2

2   2   2   2

2   2   2

2   2   2

2

Name _____

3   3   3   3

3   3   3   3

3   3   3   3

3   3   3

3   3   3

3

4   4   4   4

4   4   4   4

4   4   4   4

4   4   4

4   4   4

4

Name _____

5   5   5   5

5   5   5   5

5   5   5   5

5   5   5

5   5   5

5

Name _____

6   6   6   6

6   6   6   6

6   6   6   6

6   6   6

6   6   6

6

Name

7   7   7   7

7   7   7   7

7   7   7   7

7   7   7

7   7   7

7

Name _____

8   8   8   8

8   8   8   8

8   8   8   8

8   8   8

8   8   8

8

Name _____

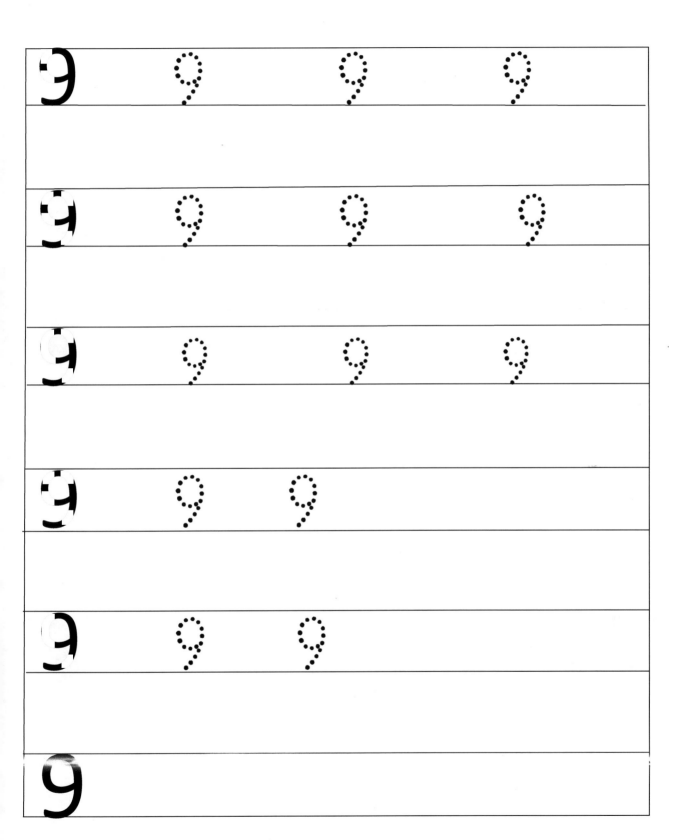

Name_____

10   10   10   10

10   10   10   10

10   10   10   10

10   10   10

10   10   10

10

Name_____

11 11 11

11 11 11

11

12 12 12

12 12 12

12

Name_____

13   13   13

13   13   13

13

14   14   14

14   14   14

14

Name _____

15   15   15

15   15   15

15

16   16   16

16   16   16

16

Name_____

17 17 17

17 17 17

17

18 18 18

18 18 18

18

Name _____

19   19   19

19   19   19

19

20   20   20

20   20   20

20

NAME _____

A a   A   a

B b   B   b

C c   C   c

D d   D   d

NAME _____

E e E e

F f F f

G g G g

H h H h

NAME _____

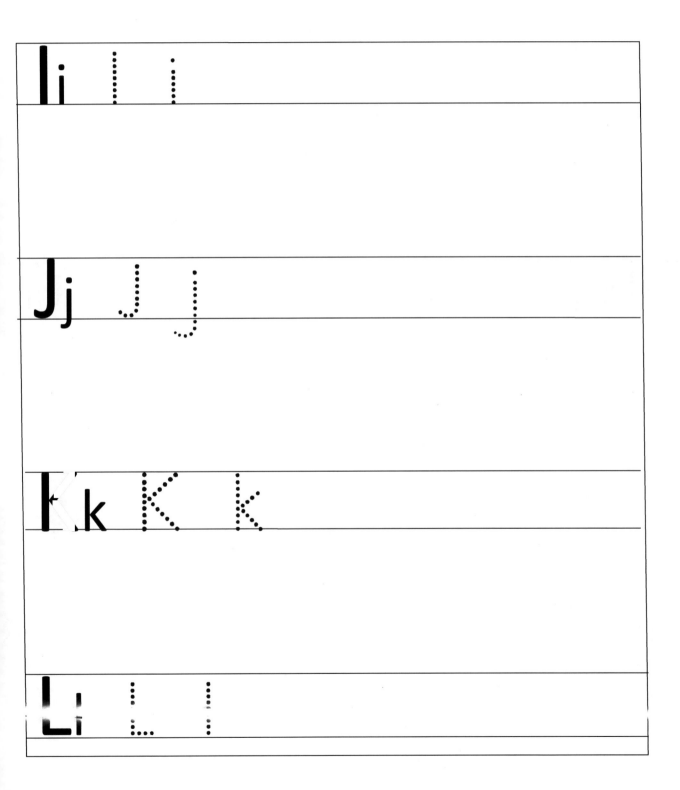

Mm M m

Nn N n

Oo O o

Pp P p

Q q   Q   q

R r   R   r

S s   S   s

T t   T   t

U u U u

V v V v

W w W w

X x X x

Yy Y y

Zz Z z

A B C D E F G H I J K

L M N O P Q R S T U

V W X Y Z

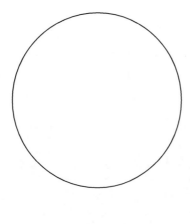

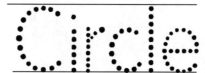

Circle

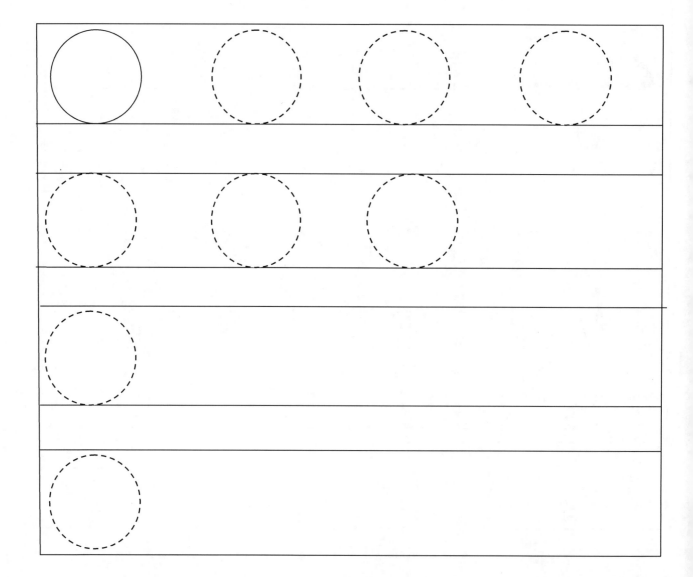

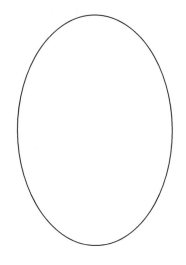

OVAL

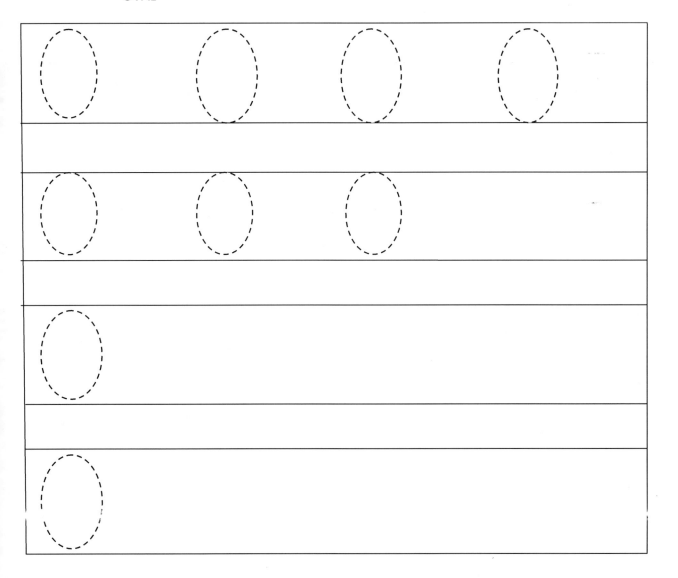

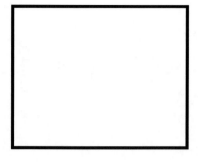

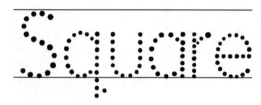

Square

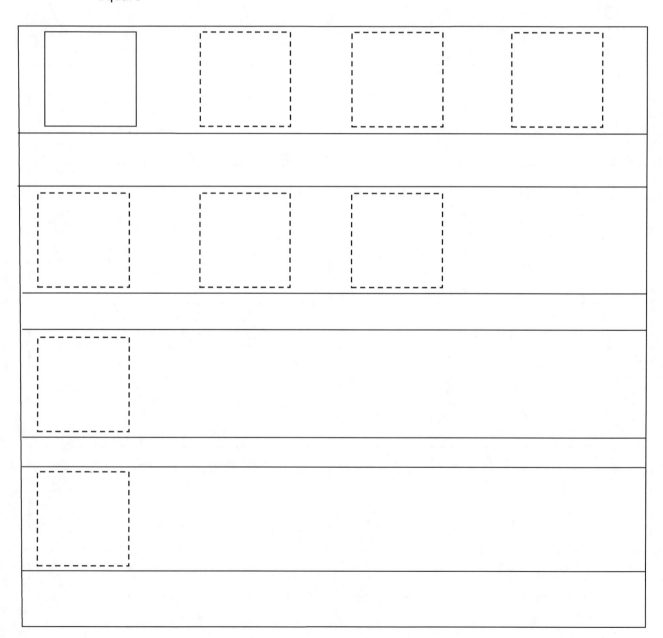

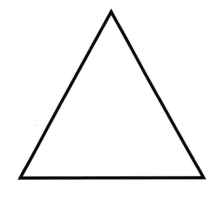

Triangle

Triangle

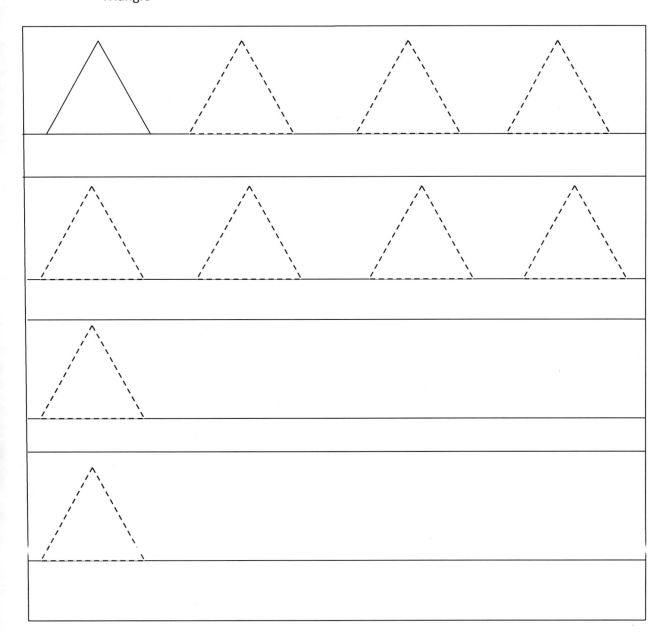

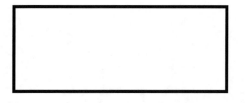

Rectangle

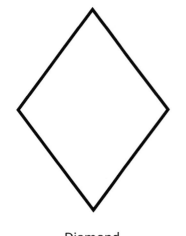

Diamond

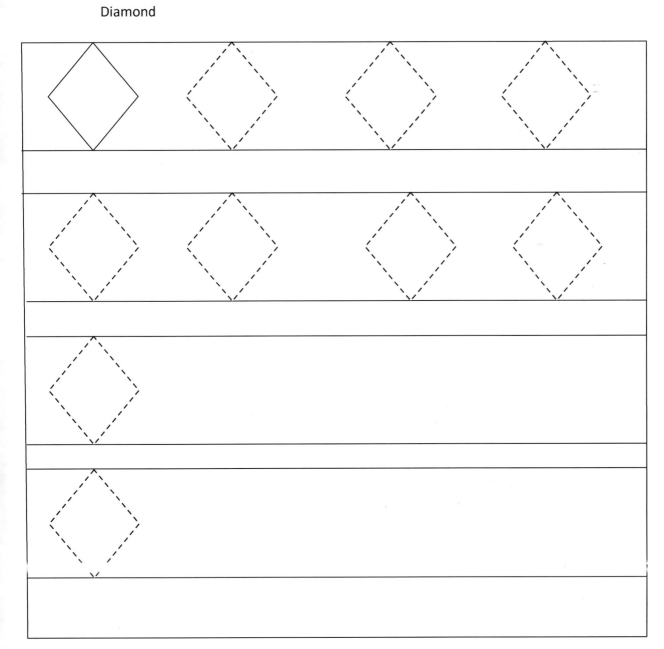

One   1   one   1

1   1   1   1

1   1   1

1

1

Two 2 two 2

2 2 2 2

2 2 2

2

2

Three   3   three   3

3   3   3   3

3   3   3

3

3

Four 4 four 4

4 4 4 4

4 4 4

4

4

Five   5   five   5

5   5   5   5

5   5   5

5

5

Six 6 six 6

6 6 6 6

6 6 6

6

6

Seven 7 seven 7

7 7 7 7

7 7 7

7

7

Eight 8   eight 8

8   8   8   8

8   8   8

8

8

Nine 9 nine 9

Ten　10　ten　10

10　　10　　10　　10

10　　10　　10

10

10

Name _____

Match the numbers

1	2
2	3
3	1
4	5
5	4

Match the numbers

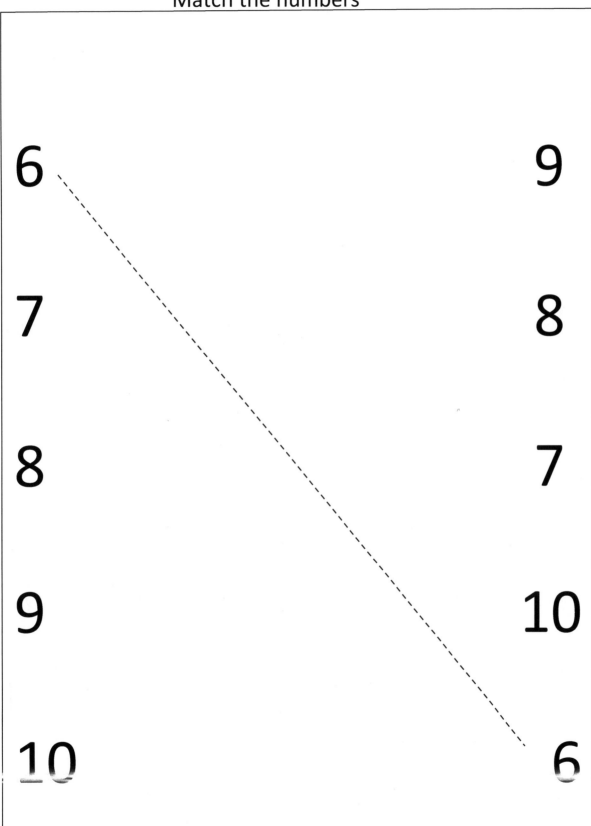

Name_____

COLOR

BLACK

BLACK

Name _____

COLOR

YELLOW

YELLOW

Name_____

BLUE

COLOR

BLUE

Name _____

COLOR

RED

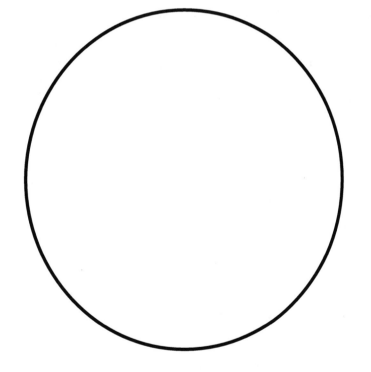

RED

Name_____

COLOR

PURPLE

PURPLE

Name_____

COLOR

BROWN

BROWN

Name_____

COLOR

ORANGE

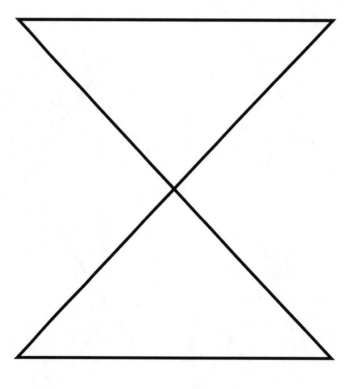

ORANGE

Name _____

COLOR

GREEN

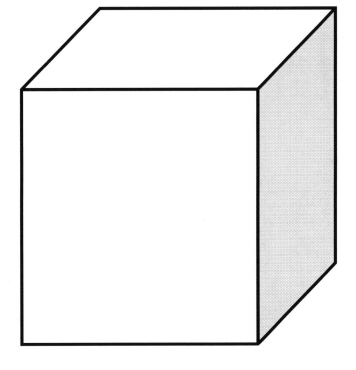

GREEN

Trace and color shape

Blue

Circle

Green

Square

Red

Triangle

Trace and color shapes

Yellow

Brown

Red

My two little hands

Did all this work.

Trace child's right hand